# Dr Korczak

David Greig was born in Edinburgh...
*The Architect, The Speculator, The Cosmonaut's Last Message to the Woman He Once Loved in the Former Soviet Union, Victoria, Outlying Islands* and *San Diego*. His work with Suspect Culture includes: *One Way Street, Airport, Timeless, Mainstream* and *Casanova*. David's translation of *Caligula* was presented at the Donmar Warehouse in an award-winning production in 2003. His work for children and young people includes: *Danny 306 + Me 4ever* and *Dr Korczak's Example*. He is dramaturg for the National Theatre of Scotland.

fairplay press

# Dr Korczak's Example

by David Greig

fairplay press

First published by Capercaillie Books Limited in 2004. This edition published by fairplay press, an imprint of Capercaillie Books Limited in 2011.

Registered office 1 Rutland Court, Edinburgh.

Printed in the UK by Marston Book Services.

A catalogue record for this book is available from the British Library.

ISBN  978-0-954520-61-8

All applications for a licence to perform this play must be made to Casarotto Ramsay & Associates Ltd., Waverley House, 7–12 Noel Street, London, W1T 8GQ. No performance may take place unless a licence has been obtained.

The publisher acknowledges support from the Scottish Arts Council towards the publication of this title.

Scottish **Arts** Council

For Lucie

# Introduction

Janusz Korczak is a much-loved writer in Poland and in many other countries of the former Eastern Bloc where generations of children have been raised on his stories. His parable about a boy who inherits a kingdom, *King Matt*, enjoys the same sort of treasured status in Eastern Europe that works like *The Lion, The Witch and The Wardrobe* do in Britain. But, for some reason, his work has never really crossed over into our Anglophone consciousness. I first came across him when the Russian theatre director Irina Brown told me of his extraordinary story and lent me translations of his novels and his diaries. I found myself immediately drawn to his work as an educator and theorist. Here was a man who in the 1930's was not only theorising about children's rights, children's courts, free-range education and work with marginalised children, but he was putting those ideas into practice in the two orphanages he ran in Warsaw. Korczak was radical then and, although some of his ideas have become central to our thinking about children, much of his thought remains radical today.

In 1998 TAG Theatre Company commissioned me to write about Korczak for a tour of secondary schools in Scotland. I wanted to use Korczak's ideas to challenge children and teachers in the heart of the very institutions which regulate children's lives. How would children in school respond to Korczak's belief that all children had a 'right' to be judged by their peers rather than only by adults? How would teachers react to Korczak's ideas about accepting children as equals?

About the right of children both to be educated and also to resist education? At a time when the New Labour government was forcing teachers to go back to rigid and disciplinarian approaches I felt that Korczak's ideas would provide an exciting counterblast – and where better to perform this than in the school gyms and assembly halls?

However, as I worked on the play I become more involved with Korczak's personal story and inevitably the shadow of the Warsaw Ghetto came to dominate my thinking. Here, it seemed to me, was the ultimate challenge to Korczak's idealism. He believed wholeheartedly in the human capacity for good and was brought into confrontation with the human capacity for the worst, most murderous, evil. Korczak's Ghetto diaries were incredibly alive with personal detail both about himself and the children. They were also full of Korczak's own attempts to understand what had brought about this calamity, this challenge to his idealism. One entry in the diary became the play's spark. Korczak writes of expelling a boy, Adzio, from the orphanage because his violence and troublemaking in the Ghetto were bringing the police to the orphanage door. In order to preserve the safety of all his children he felt forced to send the boy away. This short entry contained such a trauma, such a terrible human dilemma, that suddenly Korczak came into focus as a man.

I felt that my fictional Adzio could represent the challenge to Korczak's thinking that I needed for the drama to work. The question was this – when faced with oppression and injustice do we resist aggressively and defend ourselves like Adzio? Or, do we resist by example; by refusing to become sullied by cynicism and corruption; by appealing to the good? At last I had a question which needed a play to answer it. This was the moment I felt enabled to begin to write.

TAG are not a rich company and a schools tour is not the environment for a cast of ten, so I always knew I would have to tell my story with a small number of performers. Not for the first time in my career, necessity became the mother of dramatic invention. How could I represent the children of the orphanage? And, perhaps more importantly, how could I convey what these children suffered without descending into a tasteless and voyeuristic game of pretend. These children had existed, they had had real lives. It felt viscerally wrong of me to represent them in an unmediated way.

At the time my daughter, Annie, was four years old. I had become fascinated by the way in which she animated objects in her play – spoons, or toy animals, or furniture could be made to talk. Mr Salt Cellar could speak to Mrs Plate. Rabbit argued with Jaguar. In Annie's world, even Mr Bath had a personality and an attitude to his existence. This had no relation to puppetry. She did not require the objects to move nor did she need funny voices. She would often simply arrange her 'cast' on the kitchen table and let them begin to speak to each other. It struck me that there was an immense power in this, the simplest, form of representation. It seemed to contain the roots of theatre. I decided to try the use of simple wooden dolls. This would let me write the full range of characters. I felt it was respectful to the memory of Korczak's orphans because it would force the audience to inhabit the dolls imaginatively. Finally I hoped that I could tell the truth about the murder of these children while not forcing a young audience to confront imagery which even I, as an adult, found too painful to contemplate directly.

Since its premiere, *Dr Korczak's Example* has been performed in schools, in theatres and on the radio. It has found an audience among young people and adults. It has been translated and performed in a number of European countries. Whilst this is gratifying for me as a writer it is, I think, more a testament to the power of Korczak's ideas. His work still challenges us. It still asks questions of us that we must answer.

Shortly after completing the first draft of the play I went to spend a month in Rammalah, Palestine, working on a play for the Al Kasaba Theatre. During that period I also conducted workshops with young Palestinian writers. These workshops were organised by INAD, a children's theatre company from Bethlehem. Bethlehem and Rammalah were, at that time, under closure and the people there living in what were essentially ghettos. They faced daily humiliation and obstruction at checkpoints. There was a constant danger of violence from soldiers and settlers in the West Bank. INAD's own small theatre had been hit by a tank shell and its walls pockmarked by bullets from the settlement across the valley. Throughout this violence INAD continued their work.

I asked the company's artistic director Raeda Ghazaleh how she found the energy to work in these violent times and she spoke very movingly to me of her belief in the need to continue to behave with humanity, of continuing to show an example. I mentioned Korczak to her and to my amazement she had not only heard of the man but knew his work well. Korczak is, of course, a great hero to many in Israel. His work was almost certainly being taught in the school in the settlement across the valley from which that tank shell came. So I wondered whether Raeda might feel ambivalent towards his legacy. Raeda answered me by showing me a video of an INAD project from earlier in the year.

The young actors of INAD had gathered over a hundred children from the municipality of Beit Jala and, in the ruin of their theatre, they had set about making a banner. Then the actors and the children had marched through the ancient and scarred village to the concrete town hall on the hilltop which overlooks the valley. Once there, they demanded to be let into the hall. Finally they climbed up on to the roof and hung their banner. On the banner the children had painted the words of the United Nations Declaration of the Rights of the Child. The last image of the video shows the children cheering as the banner flutters down – its message visible across the valley: a moment which stands, for me, as a triumphant living testament to Korczak's work, and to his profound example.

**David Greig, January 2004**

# Characters

DR JANUSZ KORCZAK

ADZIO

STEPHANIE

STEPAN

A PRIEST

A NAZI OFFICER

ACTRESS

ACTOR

TOM

# Setting

The Warsaw Ghetto 1942

# Note on the Text

This play was written to be performed by three actors: an older man, a young man and a young woman. However it has already been successfully produced with a cast of five and it may be possible to experiment with larger casts in whatever configuration suits the vision of the production.

The use of dolls is important both as a stylistic device for distancing the actors and audience from the story-telling and as a way of conveying the sense of a larger canvas. The dolls do not have to be 'realistic' necessarily. Nor do they have to be puppets. They may be simple forms with significant items of dress, or decoration.

I have made suggestions in the text as to how the dolls could be used but these are nothing more than suggestions. The company must create together a production style which integrates human actors with the use of dolls. This provides many opportunities for layers of meaning. Actors in dialogue with a doll they hold in their hand, up to their face will have a different effect from actors in dialogue with a doll sitting some distance away. There are also opportunities in the moments of transformation. Dolls left in position after freezes can carry the ghost impression of scenes even while another scene is taking place.

**David Greig, May 2001**

# Scene 1

(As the audience enter:)
The sound of a playground, shouts and laughter.
On stage an array of dolls, dressed as Korczak's orphans, they are arranged in a playground scene. Some playing football, some playing other games, some reading, some smoking, some doing chores.
In the background two or three dolls are dressed as Nazi soldiers, two as Polish adults, and a Korczak doll, these figures are simply watching the playground scene.
One orphan doll, is sitting, a tiny figure in a large, real, chair in front of a real desk.
The actors enter.

ACTOR: This story happened.
   It did happen.

A siren.
A blast of martial music from the radio.

RADIO: Attention. Attention. All Jews found outside the ghetto walls without military permission will be shot. Attention. Attention.

ACTOR: The year is 1942, summer, a very hot summer that year.
   We're in Poland.
   In Warsaw, the capital.
   And we're in the Jewish Ghetto.
   All the Jewish people of Warsaw and the surrounding districts have been evicted from their homes and made to live in the new ghetto.

Three hundred and fifty thousand people crammed in to a few streets of the city. The area is surrounded by high walls and nobody is allowed in or out. Behind the walls, people try to carry on with their lives as best they can.

They look after their kids, they try to find food – which is not easy, they try to find work, which is almost impossible, they try to keep going.

All Jewish people have to wear armbands with a star on them.

Like this.

This is so that wherever you go, they can tell that you're Jewish.

And – if someone wants to insult you,

Beat you up,

Kill you,

Whatever,

They know they've got the right person.

This is an orphanage.

The orphanage is run by a man called Dr Korczak.

I'll be playing him in the story.

Dr Korczak was a real person.

But unlike me, he was bald, and he was about sixty at this time.

These kids are orphans,

They were real people, they had names.

They were pretty much like you,

But they were hungry,

Because there wasn't enough food in the Ghetto,

And most of them would have been sick as well.

**This scene may be enacted using the dolls.**

ACTOR: This is Adzio. Adzio is a character we made up – he didn't exist, but plenty kids like him did exist. Adzio's living rough on the streets of the ghetto, he's about sixteen, he's just been caught trying to steal two carrots from a stall.

POLICEMAN: You little beggar.
You thieving urchin.

ADZIO: Let me go.
Get off.

POLICEMAN: Who's your Father?

ADZIO: Don't have one.
Get off.

POLICEMAN: What am I going to do with this little thief?

ACTRESS: And what would the policeman do with Adzio?

**The policeman takes out a gun and shoots ADZIO.
The Adzio doll falls dead.**

ACTOR: That's what he would do most probably.
That's probably the truth of it.
But if we left it there,
We'd have no story would we?
So instead, we're going to lie.
We're going to make it happen like this:

**They re-enact the scene.**

POLICEMAN: You little beggar.
You thieving urchin.

ADZIO: Let me go.
Get off.

POLICEMAN: Who's your father?

ADZIO: Don't have one.
Get off.

POLICEMAN: What am I going to do with this little thief?

**Dr Korczak comes along.**

KORCZAK: Sir. Wait.
Let me take this boy.

POLICEMAN: Why should I do that? He's a thief.

KORCZAK: He's a child, sir.
If you let him come to my orphanage.
I'll see that he becomes a law-abiding citizen.
My name is Dr Korczak.

POLICEMAN: You're Dr Korczak?

KORCZAK: Please let me take the boy.

POLICEMAN: Well . . .
I shouldn't.
Thieves are to be shot, on sight.

KORCZAK: Would you like a cigarette — I happen to have a couple?

POLICEMAN: Go on then.
Get him out of my sight.

**They clear the dolls and put Adzio back in his seat.**

ACTOR: So, you see, the story didn't happen exactly the way we tell it.
Some stories — if you try and tell them exactly.
Then somehow.
You end up telling a lie.
So it didn't happen exactly the way we tell it.
But it happened.
This story happened.

**Finally, ADZIO, clears away his doll and replaces him in the chair.**

**A radio announcement:**

RADIO: Attention. Attention. All Jews found outside the ghetto walls without military permission will be shot. I repeat. All Jews found outside the ghetto walls will be shot.

**A blast of Martial Music.**

# Scene 2

**Day. Dr Korczak's office.**
**A fly is buzzing round the room.**
**ADZIO tears a strip of paper from a pad on the desk and puts it in his mouth.**
**He forms a spit ball.**
**He hurls the spitball at the fly.**
**The fly is quiet.**
**The fly buzzes again, he missed.**
**He hurls another spitball at the fly.**
**The fly is quiet.The fly buzzes again, he missed.**

ADZIO: All right.
    Fly's got brains.
    Fly's thinking.
    Fly's waiting.

**He hurls a spitball, misses.**

ADZIO: Beggar.
    Urchin.

**He hurls a spitball, misses.**

ADZIO: Fly doesn't know when to stop.
   Does he?
   Don't know when he's . . .
   *Pushing his luck fly.*

**He slaps his hand down.**
**The fly buzzes again.**

ADZIO: Bloody little shit—

**He hurls a load of spitballs in a rage.**
**Apoplectic.**
**He burns himself out.**
**Silence.**
**The fly buzzes again.**
**ADZIO offers his hand.**

ADZIO: Put it there.
   Seriously.
   Put it there.
   Fly deserves respect.
   Fly's strong, fly's wise.
   You know what – I like fly.
   Fly's cocky.
   Fly's sharp.
   Fly moves.
   Fly reminds me of me.

**The fly lands on ADZIO's hand.**

ADZIO: Fly's fly.

**Suddenly ADZIO smacks his other hand down.**
**Silence.**
**He looks between his palms.**
**Nothing.**
**The fly buzzes.**

ADZIO: War now fly.
   Fly exterminated.
   Fly wiped off the face of fly earth.
   And fly mum, and fly dad.
   And all fly friends.
   And fly wife.
   And fly kids.
   And fly aunties and fly uncles.
   I'll set fire to the world fly.
   However it happens.
   All flies die.

**He stands on the desk, fly lands. He beats the fly with roll of paper.**

ADZIO: No more fly.

**Silence.**

ADZIO: No more fly.

**Long silence.**
**STEPHANIE enters.**
**She is carrying a clipboard.**
**She sees ADZIO on the desk.**
**He sees her.**
**He gets down from the desk.**

STEPHANIE: You can sit down, if you want.

ADZIO: Why?

STEPHANIE: There's a chair, there.

ADZIO: There's an arse here, doesn't mean I have to sit on it.

STEPHANIE: Charming.

ADZIO: Who're you?

STEPHANIE: I'm Stephanie. I help Doctor Korczak. People call me Steffi.

ADZIO: Big cheese, are you?

STEPHANIE: Not really. I just need to take your details. So that you're registered as staying with us.

ADZIO: You'd make a good cop.
Face like that.
Woof Woof. Police dog.

STEPHANIE: What's your name?

**Silence.**

STEPHANIE: What's your name?

ADZIO: Fly.

STEPHANIE: No it isn't.

ADZIO: Yes it is.

STEPHANIE: You're name's Adzio.

**She writes 'Adzio' down.**

STEPHANIE: Dr Korczak told me when he brought you in.

ADZIO: Why'd you ask then?

STEPHANIE: I thought I'd try and be polite.
You could try it yourself.

ADZIO: Like your job do you, Stuffi?

STEPHANIE: Steffi.

ADZIO: Like it? The big cheesiness of it.

STEPHANIE: Mother's name?

ADZIO: Helen Damnation.

STEPHANIE: Is she alive?

ADZIO: Dead.

STEPHANIE: Father?

ADZIO: Mr Adolf Hitler of Berlin.

STEPHANIE: Father still alive?

ADZIO: Dead. Dead drunk. If he isn't dead soon I'll kill him myself.

STEPHANIE: Any brothers or sisters?

ADZIO: I had a little brother.
Misha.

STEPHANIE: What happened to him.

ADZIO: Don't ask me that.

STEPHANIE: Is he alive.

ADZIO: I said don't ask me.
I said.
All right.

STEPHANIE: Should I put down that he's dead?

ADZIO: You put down – one brother. Misha.
You put that down.
M.I.S.H.A.

STEPHANIE: Who's been looking after you, Adzio?

ADZIO: Fly.

STEPHANIE: Who's been looking after you, Fly?

ADZIO: I look after myself.

STEPHANIE: Where have you been living?

ADZIO: In the sewers.

STEPHANIE: Really?

ADZIO: Think I stink?

STEPHANIE: You can have a bath if you want.

ADZIO: I like stinking.
Don't like people getting too close.

STEPHANIE: Strip to your underwear please.

ADZIO: What?

STEPHANIE: Dr Korczak will be here soon. He's going to measure you and weigh you and give you a medical examination.

ADZIO: I'll wait, thanks.

STEPHANIE: Are you embarrassed?

ADZIO: No.

STEPHANIE: I induct all the orphans. I'm not embarrassed.

ADZIO: I'm not taking my shirt off in front of you.

STEPHANIE: Don't be childish.

**She moves to take his shirt off.**

ADZIO: Get your hands off me.

STEPHANIE: Whatever you say.
If you're going to stay here, you need to be weighed and measured. Dr Korczak needs to know how best to keep you healthy.

ADZIO: Why?

STEPHANIE: Why what?

ADZIO: Why does he want to keep me healthy?

STEPHANIE: He believes it's your right to be healthy.

ADZIO: Very nice of him.

STEPHANIE: He believes no child should be poor, or cold, or hungry.

ADZIO: What's the point.
  You're all going to die anyway.

STEPHANIE: One day.

ADZIO: One day soon. You healthy?

STEPHANIE: I'm alright. Some of the other kids are sicker.

ADZIO: Your brain's not quick though, is it.
  You're all going to die.
  You'll be transported to the east − to prisons in the forest.
  You won't come back.
  That's the word on the street.

STEPHANIE: I don't think so.

ADZIO: Germans don't care what you think.

STEPHANIE: Dr Korczak does.

ADZIO: Dr Korczak's an idiot then.

STEPHANIE: Don't you dare speak about him like that.

**KORCZAK sets up the Adzio and Stephanie dolls in the position of a slap.**

ADZIO: I speak the way I like.
  The Germans will kill you all.

STEPHANIE: Shut up.

ADZIO: Korczak's a mad old monkey.

STEPHANIE: You don't know what you're talking about.

ADZIO: Don't I?

STEPHANIE: No.

ADZIO: Not sensible am I?

STEPHANIE: No.

ADZIO: Listen to me, miss big cheese.
   They started with the beggars and the kids on the street.
   Put them on trains in the loading yard.
   I saw it. I saw it.
   It's orphans next.
   I'm only staying here until I find somewhere to run to.
   You're all dead.

STEPHANIE: Shut up. Shut up.

ADZIO: You're dead.

**STEPHANIE slaps ADZIO. Hard.**
**Music.**
**KORCZAK sets up the German soldier in the position of a sniper on the ghetto walls overlooking the orphanage.**


# Scene 3


**KORCZAK enters his office carrying bag of potatoes.**
**Some carrots.**
**He puts them down.**
**He takes money out of his pocket and counts it.**

KORCZAK: So it's your shift again is it, soldier?
   You don't need to point your gun.
   I'm going nowhere.
   Fifty zlotys.

It's late. You're like me, you work nights.

I spent the whole day trying to beg food for the children. Up and down stairs, knocking on all the doors in the ghetto. Terrible sights on the streets too.

I saw a girl of five lying dead on the pavement. Starved. Flies buzzing around her. People tried to pick their way around her where she lay.

Did you see her Soldier?

. . .

It's good to be back amongst the children.

Back to normality.

A bag of potatoes and some carrots.

Two hundred children.

It's fine.

We can make soup go.

Two hundred and one children.

We have a new boy.

He came to us today.

He calls himself—

# Scene 4

ADZIO: Fly.

KORCZAK: Fly.

STEPHANIE: His name is Adzio.

KORCZAK: Fly's fine. We'll call him Fly.

STEPHANIE: But his name is—

KORCZAK: Don't you think it's strange Stephanie that we're given our names when we're born by people who don't even know us. The name we're called every day and we can't even decide it for ourselves. Does that seem fair? Fly's fine. Fly. You can call me—

21

ADZIO: Mister Doctor Boss Sir.

KORCZAK: You can call me Dr Korczak.

ADZIO: Dr Korczak, your Majesty.
   That girl slapped me.

KORCZAK: Did you?

STEPHANIE: He said . . .

KORCZAK: What did he say?

STEPHANIE: He said you were a mad old monkey.

**KORCZAK laughs.**

KORCZAK: I like that. I prefer it to 'your Majesty' anyway.

ADZIO: Slapped me hard for it. She's dangerous.

KORCZAK: Stephanie's a tigress.

But in my experience she only gets her claws out when she's
   provoked.

ADZIO: Aren't you going to punish her?

KORCZAK: Are you going to bring a complaint?

ADZIO: I'm complaining to you, aren't I?

KORCZAK: It isn't my decision.
   You can take the case to the orphanage court if you like.

ADZIO: What?

KORCZAK: Explain your case, Stephanie will put her side of the
   story and the judges will decide a punishment.

ADZIO: You're a judge then.

KORCZAK: No. The judges are children.

ADZIO: Kids?
   They decide?

KORCZAK: If they find that you did something to provoke her, of course.

You may be punished yourself.

. . .

Stephanie. What did he say to provoke you?

STEPHANIE: Nothing. I'm sorry. It was my fault.

KORCZAK: Adzio?

ADZIO: A slap's nothing. I've had worse.

Maybe I'll leave it.

KORCZAK: It's up to you.

Stand on the scales please.

Stephanie, prepare a bed for Fly in the boys' dorm.

STEPHANIE: Yes Dr Korczak.

**ADZIO stands on the scales.**

KORCZAK: Hmm.

We'll need to feed you up.

Shirt off.

What's happened to you?

All these scars.

ADZIO: Nothing.

I got whipped.

KORCZAK: Who did this to you?

**The Adzio doll, shirt off, is sitting on the table, covered in scars.**

**KORCZAK and ADZIO examine its scars.**

ADZIO: This one was a going away present from Dad.

Uncle Moses gave me that one.

The shopkeeper on Kolodny Street kindly donated these.

Got this one when I spent a night in the cells.

. . .

Like I said your Majesty. Slap's nothing.
But I swear – anybody tries to whip me.
I'll smash their face.

KORCZAK: Nobody will whip you here, little Fly.

ADZIO: Nobody'd better – they get worse back.

KORCZAK: Let the nurse have a look at these scars.
Get yourself some soup from the kitchen.

KORCZAK: Tomorrow we'll introduce you to the other children.

ADZIO: So I'm staying am I?

KORCZAK: For now.
The orphanage is a community.
Everybody in the community has to agree to new members
joining. You'll stay here for three months.
After that, there will be a vote.
Everybody, the children, the teachers, the cleaners, the
janitor – they'll all vote on whether they find you easy to get
on with, or fine, or difficult. If nobody at all can get on with
you, then it's best you don't stay.

ADZIO: What if I don't get on with them?

KORCZAK: You're free to leave.

ADZIO: What if only a few kids get along with me?

KORCZAK: A few is fine.
Not everybody has to be popular.
But the community is more important than any individual.
So the community decides.

ADZIO: Yeah – but really – you're the boss. It's your place – you
tell them what to do.

KORCZAK: Really I don't.

ADZIO: . . .

**KORCZAK laughs.**

KORCZAK: I'm just a mad old monkey.
   The children decide what happens round here.

ADZIO: You let kids tell you what to do?
   That's crazy.

KORCZAK: What would you do, Fly?
   If you had power?

ADZIO: I don't.

KORCZAK: But if you did?
   Say you were – king.

ADZIO: King of Poland?

KORCZAK: King of the world.

ADZIO: King of the world. Me?

KORCZAK: You.

**He gives ADZIO the doll.**
**ADZIO takes the doll. He stands it on the desk.**

ADZIO: King Aadzio the Fly.
   I'd get them to make me a plane.
   And I'd buzz around in it.

KORCZAK: What else.

ADZIO: I'd get them to make me a very comfortable bed.
   Which I'd never get out of.
   And I'd have slaves.

**KORCZAK brings some other dolls, to be his slaves.**

ADZIO: Bring me a breakfast of:
    Ham and – more ham.
    And some eggs.
    Some beer.
    Some jam.
    Some beef and–
    And some more ham.

**The slave dolls bring dinner.**

SLAVE: Are you going to get out of bed today sire?

ADZIO: No.

SLAVE: Very good sire.

KORCZAK: What else?

ADZIO: I'd have an army.

KORCZAK: Who would they fight?

ADZIO: Anyone who tried to get me.
    I'd get rid of the Germans for a start.

**KORCZAK brings another doll.**

GENERAL: General Korczak – reporting for duty.
    We attacked the Germans yesterday.
    We won a great victory.
    They are defeated.

ADZIO: Good work, General.
    Bring me a German prisoner.

GENERAL: As you wish sire.

**KORCZAK brings a Nazi doll.**
**ADZIO considers the doll.**

ADZIO: Skin him. Skin him alive.

KORCZAK: You show no mercy?

ADZIO: None.
    Bring more. More Germans.

KORCZAK: But the Germans are already defeated.

ADZIO: Bring them all.
    I want to watch them skinned.

KORCZAK: Is there nothing else I can bring you, that would bring you pleasure?

ADZIO: A warm bed I don't ever have to get out of.

KORCZAK: What about laws? Aren't you going to make some laws?

ADZIO: Tell everyone to go and hang themselves.

ADZIO: Now leave me alone.
    Just leave me alone.

KORCZAK: As you wish sire.

**The dolls are taken away. The Adzio doll is left on the desk.**

KORCZAK: The boys' dorm is on the first floor.
    Really it's just a classroom full of mattresses.
    I'm sorry your palace isn't more comfortable, your Majesty.
    But – that's the way things are these days.
    If you go to the kitchen, Maria will give you some soup.

ADZIO: I said leave me alone.

KORCZAK: Welcome to the community, Fly.

**He goes to shake hands with ADZIO. ADZIO doesn't shake hands. ADZIO exits. The doll is left on the desk.**

# Scene 5

**KORCZAK puts the Adzio doll to bed. He puts the other
dolls to bed.**

KORCZAK: It's ten o'clock.
Everyone's in bed.
Me – like you, soldier, I'm awake.

**Suddenly shots ring out.
KORCZAK ducks under the table.
He goes to the window.
Looks.**

KORCZAK: Hey!
Why are you shooting!

**Another shot.
KORCZAK remains where he is.**

KORCZAK: People are trying to get some sleep in here.
Have some consideration.

**Silence.**

KORCZAK: Maybe you don't like to sleep at night?
Why do we obey clocks, soldier? Do you know?
. . .
Me neither. It's ridiculous when you think about it.
I prefer to sleep in the day.
Bread and water taste better at night.
Don't you agree?
Well. Goodnight.

**He sits at his desk.**

**He has a glass of water and a hunk of bread.**
**A knock.**

KORCZAK: Come in.

**STEPHANIE enters.**

KORCZAK: Stephanie.

STEPHANIE: I couldn't sleep.
I saw your light was burning.
Did you hear the shooting?

KORCZAK: I heard it.

STEPHANIE: Do you mind if I – keep you company?

KORCZAK: I'd welcome it.
Do you want some bread?

STEPHANIE: No thank you.

**She sits.**

STEPHANIE: I won't disturb you.
I'll just sit.

**KORCZAK starts writing in a notebook.**

STEPHANIE: What are you writing?

KORCZAK: Notes about the children.

STEPHANIE: You write about us?

KORCZAK: Not your secrets, just what you tell me.

KORCZAK: Zygmus – a worrying boil on his leg.
He was upset today because another boy insulted his sister.
Sami – Sami wants to keep a goldfinch.
I told him all the finches were gone from the Ghetto because

people have either eaten them, or let them fly away because
they can't afford to keep them.
He seemed unhappy.
Abrasza – Abrasza has lost the key to his locker.
I asked the Janitor to open it for him.
Adzio – ah, Adzio . . .

# Scene 6

**Night in the boys' dormitory.**
**The Adzio doll gets out of bed, sneaks over to another boy's
bed, steals a piece of bread.**
**ADZIO eats the bread.**

ADZIO: Fly's hungry.
　　Fly eats.
　　Fly's full.
　　Fly sleeps.

**The Adzio doll goes to sleep.**

# Scene 7

**KORCZAK and STEPHANIE, as before.**

KORCZAK: Adzio seems . . . on the edge of something.
　　On the edge of a cliff?
　　On a razor's edge?
　　I hope we can bring him back.
　　Stephanie – what shall I write about Stephanie?
　　Stephanie seems worried.

STEPHANIE: Me. No?

KORCZAK: Is it the shooting.

STEPHANIE: It's nothing.

KORCZAK: Are you sure?

STEPHANIE: Certain.

KORCZAK: I'll make a bargain with you.
 I'll tell you what's worrying me, if you tell me what's worrying you.

STEPHANIE: What's worrying you, Dr Korczak?

KORCZAK: In a few months it will be winter.
 We'll need coal.
 I don't know where we'll find it.

STEPHANIE: Oh.

KORCZAK: We'll manage.
 It'll be fine.
 All's fine.

STEPHANIE: Dr Korczak.
 Will we still be here in the winter?

KORCZAK: Why shouldn't we be?

STEPHANIE: Adzio said—

KORCZAK: Yes—

STEPHANIE: Adzio said we're going to be killed.

KORCZAK: Did he?

STEPHANIE: He said in two weeks.

KORCZAK: That's what's worrying you?

STEPHANIE: The shooting — Adzio's right, isn't he?
 They made us wear these armbands.

Then they moved us into the Ghetto.
Then they stopped us travelling anywhere.
And now . . .
Now they . . .

KORCZAK: These are very bad times Stephanie.
I can't pretend it isn't like it is.

STEPHANIE: Are they going to—

KORCZAK: Do you think so?

STEPHANIE: Do you?

KORCZAK: No.

STEPHANIE: How do you know?

KORCZAK: Because . . .
Because I don't see any reason why the Germans would want
to do such a thing.

STEPHANIE: They put us in the Ghetto.

KORCZAK: They don't like Jews. They've made that clear.
They think we're a nuisance but —
I don't believe anybody is capable of —
No.

STEPHANIE: Do you promise?

KORCZAK: I promise.

**STEPHANIE gets up to leave.**

STEPHANIE: Goodnight Dr Korczak.

KORCZAK: Stephanie?

STEPHANIE: Yes.

KORCZAK: What do you make of Adzio?

STEPHANIE: I think he's . . .

KORCZAK: Be honest.

STEPHANIE: I think he's rough.

KORCZAK: Do you like him?

STEPHANIE: No.


# Scene 8

**Morning. The orphanage canteen.**

KORCZAK: Attention everybody. Attention please.
Before you all go off to classes, I have an announcement to make. The house is infested with flies. It's high summer and the flies are getting everywhere, and they're spreading disease and making us get sick. So the Orphanage Council have passed a new rule. Before you can go to the toilet you have to kill a certain number of flies — five flies for a number one, fifteen for a number two. Is that clear? That way we'll have the flies under control in a week or two.

ADZIO: Mad old monkey.

STEPHANIE: Dr Korczak — I'm bursting.

KORCZAK: Then you'd better hurry up and catch some flies.

STEPHANIE: But—

KORCZAK: Five flies. That's the rule.


**STEPHANIE begins – flies buzzing – she struggles – she isn't very good at it.**

ADZIO: Wait, Stuffi, you go and pee.
I'll catch your flies for you.

STEPHANIE: Thank you.

**STEPHANIE exits.**
**Music.**
**The flies buzz.**
**One by one Adzio picks them off.**
**Beautifully, almost balletically.**

ADZIO: One. Two. Three. Four. Five.

**When he's finished, KORCZAK applauds.**

KORCZAK: Well done.

ADZIO: It's easy work. I just imagine they're Germans.

KORCZAK: I didn't mean well done for catching flies.
  I meant well done for helping Steffi.

ADZIO: I don't help nobody except myself.

KORCZAK: No. Of course you don't.

# Scene 9

**Afternoon. Dr Korczak' office.**

STEPHANIE: Dr Korczak, you have a visitor

**Stepan enters.**

KORCZAK: Stepan! My friend. What are you doing here?

STEPAN: I bribed a guard at the gates of the Ghetto. I don't have
  long.

KORCZAK: Stepan, you're in danger. Christian Poles aren't

allowed in the Ghetto. You can be shot.

STEPAN: I know Janusz. These are such dangerous times.
I heard they'd put you in prison.

KORCZAK: Only for a week. I refused to wear their armband.

STEPAN: It must have been terrible.

KORCZAK: I enjoyed it.
I had time to write.
Time to tell stories.

STEPAN: This isn't a time for stories anymore.
In the past things were less serious.
Look – I have a false passport. I can get you out of the Ghetto.
I can get you to Palestine.
Please – save yourself.

KORCZAK: What about the children?

STEPAN: We can work something out – hide them with Polish families.
Maybe we can hide them in the monasteries.

KORCZAK: I can't have the children locked in dark cellars always terrified of being discovered.

STEPAN: They might be safer than here.

KORCZAK: Can you guarantee their safety?

STEPAN: Of course not. I can't guarantee my own safety.

KORCZAK: I can't leave the children.

STEPAN: You must.

KORCZAK: I can't abandon them.
I don't want to.
It would be desertion.

They've all been deserted by their parents.
I can't do that to them again.

STEPAN: The Nazis are tightening a noose around you.
You have a chance to escape.
You're an important man.
I beg you to take it.

KORCZAK: No.
Tell me Stepan, when you came here, did you think I would say yes to your plan?

STEPAN: No.

**They embrace.**

KORCZAK: They won't kill us.
Life will be hard,
But they won't kill us.
We must carry on. We must show them how to live.
That's how we fight them. Stepan. Every time a Christian like you embraces a Jew like me we're fighting back.

**Stepan leaves.**

# Scene 10

**STEPHANIE returns carrying a clipboard.**

STEPHANIE: I have the court cases for the week, Dr Korczak.

KORCZAK: Thank you Stephanie, put them on my desk.

STEPHANIE: There's a new case. Just in this morning.

**Korczak reads.**

KORCZAK: Oh dear. Adzio.

STEPHANIE: Bruno says Adzio stole his bread in the night. Bruno's furious. He was saving the bread for his kid brother. I told you he was rough.

KORCZAK: Very well.
We'll hold the court this afternoon.

**ADZIO bursts in.**

ADZIO: Hey boss, one of the kids told me I've got to go to some court thing.

KORCZAK: Bruno says you stole his bread.

ADZIO: And you believe him?

KORCZAK: The court will decide, on the evidence.

ADZIO: I'm not scared of a bunch of kids.

KORCZAK: A children's court might seem strange to you now Adzio.
But I promise you, in fifty years' time, when you're an old man, every school, every children's home will have one.
A child has the right to be judged by people his own age.

ADZIO: If you think I stole the mongrel's bread why don't you just give me a whipping?

KORCZAK: Because I believe in justice.
ADZIO: There's a German with a gun out there.
Put him in your court.
See what happens.
You got a gun too?
Who cares about your court?

**ADZIO exits.**

# Scene 11

**KORCZAK bangs a gavel on his desk.**

KORCZAK: Today's judges are . . .

**He picks names out of a hat.**

KORCZAK: Jerzy
Miriam
Coco
and
Jakob.

**He places the doll judges (Bruno and Tadeusz) on the table. He places Adzio in front of them.**

KORCZAK: Lets hear the evidence. Bruno . . .

BRUNO: Last night I had some bread out beside my bed. I was saving it to give to my brother in the morning. When I woke up this morning it was gone. Tadeusz said he saw Adzio take it.

KORCZAK: Tadeusz. Did you see him?

TADEUSZ: I saw him.

KORCZAK: Adzio – how do you plead? Guilty or not guilty?

ADZIO: What difference does it make?
It's all a joke.

KORCZAK: Do you have anything to say?

ADZIO: No.

KORCZAK: No defence at all?
Does anybody have anything to say on ADZIO's behalf?
. . .

Nobody will speak for him?

Stephanie?

A hungry child, comes straight in from the street, he hardly knows the rules of the orphanage – the only rules he knows are the ones that mean you survive out there – and nobody will speak for him?

STEPHANIE: . . . He caught flies for me this morning.

KORCZAK: An act of kindness. So – Anyone else?

. . .

Judges? You have the evidence. What is your verdict?

**He bangs the gavel.**
**STEPHANIE reads out the verdict.**

STEPHANIE: Guilty.

Adzio – your sentence is to give Bruno your bread ration for the next three days.

ADZIO: You'll see if we're still here in three days.

Let him have my bread.

I don't care.

STEPHANIE: Next Case.

**He bangs the Gavel.**

# Scene 12

**KORCZAK and the Soldier.**
**KORCZAK is enraged.**
**He sets up a football match in the playground with the dolls.**

KORCZAK: What kind of poison are you spilling into their heads, Soldier?

You and your gun and your armbands and your bloody Ghetto.

We had a court. The children respected it.

Now they only see justice coming from a gun.

We had a newspaper. The children wrote it.

Now they don't even read it because the only thing they want to know is what's to become of them.

And only you can tell them that.

So what?

What next?

Soldier!

Soldier!

What next for us?

What next?

**The Soldier does not reply.**
**KORCZAK blows a whistle.**

# Scene 13

**A football game. ADZIO is on the sidelines, watching. KORCZAK approaches him.**

KORCZAK: Don't you want to play football?

ADZIO: No.

KORCZAK: Can you play?

ADZIO: I play. My brother's better.

He's got magic feet.

Ball sticks to him.

He could be professional.

KORCZAK: Where is your brother?

ADZIO: . . .

KORCZAK: Why don't you play? It might cheer you up.

ADZIO: You want me to play.
    I'll play.

**ADZIO runs. Gets the ball. Hacks, pushes and cheats his way to the goalmouth. Pushes the goalkeeper over. And scores.**

ADZIO: One nil.

**He cheers himself.**
**But he is doing it without joy.**
**He walks away from the group and back to his sitting position.**

ADZIO: I can play.
    I can score.
    If that's what you want.

KORCZAK: That wasn't playing. That was cheating.

ADZIO: The ball went in the net.
    That's what counts.

KORCZAK: The way you played. It was unfair. You pushed – you hacked. You broke all the rules.

ADZIO: And I scored.

KORCZAK: Did it make you happy to score?

ADZIO: Who says it's supposed to?
    Look, old man.
    You don't get it, do you?

41

You think your rules and your courts and your whatever is
supposed to impress me?
You're either blind or stupid.
Out there – in the world.
You want something – you take it.
You got something – you fight to keep it.
You steal.
You rob.
You cheat.
And you don't feel bad about it.
Because if you don't do it to them.
They'll do it to you.
My brother was like you –
Look where it got him.

KORCZAK: Where did it get him?

ADZIO: I scored. That's all.

KORCZAK: Perhaps you're right.

ADZIO: I know what people are like.

KORCZAK: I know what children are like.

ADZIO: You know what these soft kids are like.
Out there – in the street.
They wouldn't survive one minute.
If a German sniper doesn't get them, then a gang of Jews will
steal their money, their clothes, their food.
And if they don't, then they'll starve anyway, because they'll
be too proud to beg and too stupid to steal.
I will be alive.

KORCZAK: You'll be alive.
But . . .
In a world like that.
What would be the point?

**KORCZAK leaves ADZIO.**
**STEPHANIE approaches ADZIO.**
**ADZIO doesn't say anything.**

STEPHANIE: . . .

ADZIO: What?

STEPHANIE: I came to say thank you, for catching the flies for
me today.

ADZIO: Is that why you spoke up for me in the court?

STEPHANIE: I spoke because I wanted to.

ADZIO: I can speak for myself, you know.

STEPHANIE: I know.
Can I sit with you?
I hate football as well.

ADZIO: Do what you like.

STEPHANIE: You're funny. You know that?

ADZIO: No I'm not.

STEPHANIE: Yes you are.
You talk like a gangster.
But – you look like a . . .
Like a rabbit or something.
Twitchy and soft.

ADZIO: Get lost.

**She does a rabbit impression.**

ADZIO: I'll smash your face in.

**She does the impression again.**

ADZIO: Stop it.

**She does it again.**

STEPHANIE: I don't know why you're upset.
    I like rabbits.
    I like their little tufty heads.

**She musses up his hair.**
**He won't look at her.**

STEPHANIE: You're smiling. I can see.
    Gangsters don't smile.
    You'd better not let anyone see you smile.
    They might not be scared of you anymore.

**STEPHANIE walks away.**
**Before STEPHANIE leaves the scene she turns.**
**She does a rabbit impression at him.**

STEPHANIE: Now I know why you were stealing carrots.

**ADZIO stands up, leaves his doll in his place.**
**A look between actor and actress.**

# Scene 14

**KORCZAK is putting his coat on, his hat, a tie. He smartens himself up.**

KORCZAK: A long time ago, Soldier,
    when I was a young man.
    The Prime Minister was drunk after lunch in a pub.
    And a journalist asked him about the state of the country.
    And he said —
    It's fine. It's all fine.

The harvest had failed and there were riots in the streets.
But the Prime Minister said:
It's fine, it's all fine.
And now it seems I'm saying it.
My children are starving –
It's fine, it's all fine.
In the Ghetto we're all sleepwalkers.
You've made us into zombies, Soldier.
It's fine.
It's all fine.
I'm going to see Adam Cerniakov tonight.
If you're meeting the leader of the Jews – you have to look the part.

**A Cerniakov doll.**

KORCZAK: Adam.

CERNIAKOV: Dr Korczak! Janusz. Good to see you. What can I do for you?

KORCZAK: I want to know what's to happen to the children.

CERNIAKOV: In what way, Janusz?

KORCZAK: There are rumours.

CERNIAKOV: You don't have to tell me about rumours. They're thicker than flies these days.

KORCZAK: Rumours that the children have heard.

CERNIAKOV: Yes.

KORCZAK: That they're to be . . .

CERNIAKOV: What?

KORCZAK: That the Germans intend to . . .
Intend to . . .

CERNIAKOV: Oh. That rumour.

KORCZAK: Well . . . what do you know about it?

CERNIAKOV: Look, I deal with the Germans.
I run the Ghetto for them.
People don't like me for it, I don't like myself for it most of the time.
But if someone has to organise this hell hole I'd rather it was me than them.

KORCZAK: What is to happen to my orphans?

CERNIAKOV: I can't say the Germans are kind, Janusz.
Or that they don't despise us.
But they're human, nonetheless.
They don't plan to − not the children −
I can promise you that.

KORCZAK: I have your word.

CERNIAKOV: You do.

**They shake hands.**

KORCZAK: It's getting worse every day, Adam.

CERNIAKOV: I'm doing my best to . . . make it less bad.

KORCZAK: I worry about you.

CERNIAKOV: About me?

KORCZAK: You're a good man, Adam.
I worry about your soul.
Trading, haggling with these people.

CERNIAKOV: What else do you suggest I do?
How can we resist them?

KORCZAK: By example.
We could show them how to live.

We demonstrate that we do not accept that the world is the way they say it is.

CERNIAKOV: And in the meantime starve.
It's blind idealism, Janusz.

KORCZAK: I don't know.
Sometimes I want to take the children and just march them out.
Under the green flag.
And we'll march all the way to the summer camp at Little Rose.
Just see if they stop us.

CERNIAKOV: They would stop you.
They would kill you.

KOCZAK: But we would have shown them we're not animals.

CERNIAKOV: I promise I'll keep the children safe.

KORCZAK: Thank you.

CERNIAKOV: You're doing a good job, Janusz.
You resist them your way. I'll resist them my way.
Maybe one of us will make a difference.

**KORCZAK leaves the doll.**

# Scene 15

**Korczak at his desk.**
**STEPHANIE is with him.**

STEPHANIE: Is everything all right, Dr Korczak?

KORCZAK: It's fine,

All fine.

What can I do for you?

STEPHANIE: I brought you a note – it's from some of the older boys.

They wonder if you would deliver it?

KORCZAK: What does it say?

STEPHANIE: 'To the Vicar of All Saints Church.

We kindly request permission to come to the church garden for a little while on Saturday. In the morning. Early if possible. The Germans have stopped us from visiting Little Rose. We long for air and greenery. It is stuffy and crowded where we are. We'd like to see nature again. We promise not to damage the plants. Please don't say no.

Yours,

Sami

Zygmus

Aronek

Abrasza

and

Hanka.'

What should we do?

KORCZAK: Good. An excellent idea.

Take the note to the Vicar.

You take it – you and . . . Adzio. You go.

STEPHANIE: Adzio?

KORCZAK: Yes.

Go.

Go now.

**STEPHANIE leaves.**
**KORCZAK is alone.**

KORCZAK: I've trained them well.
For a perfect world.
How will they survive this one?

# Scene 16

**STEPHANIE and ADZIO walking through the streets of the Ghetto, carrying the note.**

STEPHANIE: You should see Little Rose, Adzio, you'd love it.
We used to go every July and we all lived there together in the bunkhouses. We built them ourselves. We kept horses and pigs and a few cows. And we picked blackberries. And we went swimming in the river.

ADZIO: The countryside.
Never been myself.
Don't think I'd like it.
I'm a city boy.

STEPHANIE: Why wouldn't you like it?

ADZIO: No shops.
Where'd I steal my food?

STEPHANIE: The country's nothing to be afraid of.
When we go again, you can come.

ADZIO: Yeah.

STEPHANIE: You'll like it.

ADZIO: If you like the country so much.
Maybe this'll remind you of it.

**He gives her an apple.**

STEPHANIE: Where did you get this?

ADZIO: Pinched it. Didn't I?

STEPHANIE: I can't eat it if you stole it.

ADZIO: Why not?

STEPHANIE: It'd be . . . mind you . . . it does look good.

ADZIO: How else you gonna get an apple round here?

STEPHANIE: It's still stolen, Adzio.
   Well.

**She bites the apple.**

ADZIO: How's it taste?

STEPHANIE: Good.
   It tastes good.
   Have a bite.

**ADZIO takes a bite.**

ADZIO: Hits the spot.
   Let's sit here for a bit.
   It's too hot to run errands.
   We'll get there in the end.

**They sit.**

ADZIO: Used to sit here with my brother.
   Used to watch him play football in the street.
   Used to be a crowd would come and watch him.
   Could play for Poland one day.
   That's what they'd say.

STEPHANIE: Where is he now? Your brother?

ADZIO: In the country.

**A Musician approaches.**
**He is playing for them.**
**Begging from them.**

ADZIO: Here you go –
 I knew he'd come along –
 Can't have dinner without an orchestra, can you?

STEPHANIE: Who's he?

ADZIO: A friend of mine.

STEPHANIE: He's really good.

ADZIO: He used to be famous – he still is – he's played all over
 Europe.
 Played in the opera house in Paris he has.
 Now he has to sing for his supper same as the rest of us.

STEPHANIE: I haven't heard music for ages.

ADZIO: Hey Tom.
 Tom – give us a tune.
 None of that opera house stuff.
 Nothing sad.
 Something to cheer us up.

**He takes another apple out of his pocket and throws it to**
**the Musician, who catches it.**

ADZIO: I was busy this morning.

**TOM begins to play a fast, cheerful tune.**
**STEPHANIE is enjoying it.**
**She stands up.**

STEPHANIE: C'mon –

ADZIO: What?

STEPHANIE: Let's dance

ADZIO: I can't.

STEPHANIE: 'Course you can.

ADZIO: Legs made of wood these.
    Never got taught.

STEPHANIE: It's easy.

ADZIO: No – I look stupid.

STEPHANIE: You look good.

ADZIO: No.

STEPHANIE: You do. Come on.

**He gets up. They dance together. A waltz perhaps.
STEPHANIE looks at the Musician.
He slows the music down.
They dance together more slowly.
The music comes to an end.
STEPHANIE kisses ADZIO.
(More than a peck.)
She sits down.**

STEPHANIE: Thank you, Fly.

**He stands a moment.
He sits down too.**

ADZIO: We should . . . we . . .
    Should be . . . getting on.

STEPHANIE: You're embarrassed.

ADZIO: No.

STEPHANIE: Didn't expect that, did you?

ADZIO: No.

STEPHANIE: I'll let you into a secret.
Neither did I.

ADZIO: Was it . . . was it — I haven't — that — done it before.

STEPHANIE: Never kissed?

ADZIO: No.

STEPHANIE: I give you five.

ADZIO: Out of five?

STEPHANIE: Out of ten — big head.

ADZIO: Oh.

STEPHANIE: If you want to get better marks, you'll just have to practise.
Let's go and find this priest.

**They exit.**

# Scene 17

**Korczak and the Soldier.**

KORCZAK: I'm watering my plants.
Some flowers, a window box.
You see how normal things are round here, Soldier.
Flowers in the summer.
I look out of my window and I can smell the countryside.
I can see the forest.
I refuse to see walls.
I refuse to see guns.
Point your gun if you like.

Shoot.
What do you see, Soldier?
The inside of your own head.
I would like to see that.
That would give me nightmares.

**The Soldier shoots.**
**Misses.**
**Korczak doesn't flinch.**

# Scene 18

**ADZIO and STEPHANIE are with the PRIEST.**
**The PRIEST looks at the letter.**

PRIEST: No.

ADZIO: What?

PRIEST: I'm terribly sorry.

STEPHANIE: But father . . .

ADZIO: No?

PRIEST: I'm afraid . . . it's really . . . out of the question.

STEPHANIE: We promise not to damage anything.

ADZIO: No Jews in your garden – is that it?

PRIEST: I'd love to be able to help. Believe me.
But . . . in these times . . . it's hard enough.
My congregation can't even come to their own church
because it's here in the Ghetto.

ADZIO: So the garden isn't being used.
It's going to waste.

We could look after it.

PRIEST: I just don't think the church ought to be . . .

ADZIO: Helping Jews.

PRIEST: Drawing attention to ourselves.

ADZIO: They're just kids.
    They want to breathe fresh air.

PRIEST: Look – the Church looks after Christians.
    Go to the damn synagogue if you want fresh air.

STEPHANIE: There are no other gardens in the Ghetto.

PRIEST: I'm sorry.

ADZIO: No your not.

PRIEST: Don't talk back to me.

ADZIO: You fat toad.
    Look at you – smug – plopped down on the riverbank
    Catching flies.

STEPHANIE: Adzio, don't.

ADZIO: Big fat stomach full.
    Them kids are starving. They got nothing.
    And you won't even let them borrow your fresh air.

PRIEST: Get out.

ADZIO: Fat toad on a stone.
    I hope the Germans get you.

PRIEST: Go.

ADZIO: Come on, Steffi.

STEPHANIE: Please father, won't you reconsider?

PRIEST: Out before I call the Gestapo.

ADZIO: Don't need to call them, toad.
　　They're already here.
　　They've got an office in your head.

**ADZIO and STEPHANIE leave.**
**Outside the church.**

STEPHANIE: You shouldn't have shouted at him.

**ADZIO ignores her.**

STEPHANIE: He might have changed his mind.

**ADZIO ignores her.**

STEPHANIE: You just made him angry.

**ADZIO picks up a stone and in a single movement hurls**
**itthrough the church windows.**
**The smashing of glass.**

ADZIO: He made me angry.
　　What about you?
　　How angry are you?

**ADZIO gives her a stone.**
**She considers.**
**She throws.**
**Another smash.**

ADZIO: Good isn't it!

STEPHANIE: It's brilliant.

ADZIO: Wish I had a gun.

**Another smash.**

# Scene 19

**ADZIO and STEPHANIE are sitting in KORCZAK's room.**

KORCZAK: I'm very disappointed in you.
  Both of you.
  You should know better, Stephanie.

STEPHANIE: He deserved it.

KORCZAK: You threw a stone at a church.

STEPHANIE: He wouldn't let us use the garden.

KORCZAK: He won't now, will he?

ADZIO: You don't get it, do you?
  We can be nice to him. We can beg and plead.
  He'll never let us into his garden.
  Because we're Jews.
  And because he thinks we're nothing.

KORCZAK: So you stone him?

ADZIO: Yes.
  We fight.

KORCZAK: A fight you're bound to lose.

ADZIO: Maybe.

KORCZAK: And worse. Now we'll have complaints. We'll have
  police coming to our door. They'll come after you two, after
  all of us. You've put the whole orphanage in danger with your
  . . . big gesture.

STEPHANIE: I'm sorry, Dr Korczak.

ADZIO: No you're not. She's not sorry.

KORCZAK: Stephanie?

STEPHANIE: I'm sorry that I've made trouble.
>But.
>Adzio's right.
>I'm not sorry for throwing a stone at his church.
>It felt good.

KORCZAK: This'll have to go to the court, you know.
>Bringing danger to us all.
>You could be expelled.

ADZIO: You love your court, don't you?

KORCZAK: It's your court too.

ADZIO: It's not a court, it's a joke.
>We're kids.
>We're orphans.
>In a ghetto.
>The Germans are the bosses.
>Why play pretend games?
>The only power we've got's our fists, stones – the knives in the kitchen . . .

KORCZAK: If there is no justice out there in the world, then our court is the only true justice left.
>How dare you endanger it?

ADZIO: Call Adolf Hitler before your kiddie court.
>See what happens.

KORCZAK: Adzio.
>We have to protect our community.
>Every time you cause trouble you're bringing danger to us.

ADZIO: Every time the sun comes up it brings danger.
>Every time the sun goes down the danger's worse.
>At least I fight back.

KORCZAK: We fight too.
>By proving that justice, and honesty, and tolerance still exist.

We will resist the Nazis.

ADZIO: Difference is, they don't care about your example, Dr Korczak.

They'll care about my knife in their back though.

**ADZIO leaves.**
**KORCZAK puts his head in his hands.**

STEPHANIE: If it weren't for you, Dr Korczak, and for the home.
I would never have known that there are honest people in the world.
That I can tell the truth. That there is justice.
But I do know.
So when I saw that priest, I was more angry.
Because I expected him to be good.
You're a saint, Dr Korczak. You can restrain yourself.
But I can't.
I'm sorry.

**STEPHANIE leaves.**
**KORCZAK is tired and depressed.**
**He turns to the Soldier.**

KORCZAK: Who are you?
Look at you – hardly more than a boy.
A boy with a gun.
Maybe you're an apprentice mechanic from Leipzig.
Maybe you like dancing.
Maybe you've got a girl back home – or here even.
Maybe you're an orphan.
I'd like to meet you.
Meanwhile.
My bald head is glinting in the moonlight.
Your target.
Sometimes I wish you'd just shoot.

# Scene 20

**STEPHANIE in bed.**
**ADZIO enters.**
**ADZIO wakes Stephanie.**

STEPHANIE: What — What is it?

ADZIO: Shhh.
Don't wake the others.

STEPHANIE: You're not supposed to be here.

ADZIO: Not supposed to be in lots of places, am I?
But I go.
Rules don't stop me.
You not pleased to see me?

STEPHANIE: 'Course I am.

ADZIO: I want you to come with me.
Now.

STEPHANIE: Where to?

ADZIO: The streets.

STEPHANIE: I can't go back on the streets. I couldn't bear it.

ADZIO: Look — there's other ones like us in the Ghetto.
Ones who know what's coming.
And they want to fight back.
Tom — the musician — he told me.
They're organising an uprising.
I heard about them.
They're going to rise up and fight their way out.

STEPHANIE: What are you talking about?

ADZIO: A proper fight — not just throwing stones.
Look — I stole this from the kitchens.

**ADZIO shows her a knife.**

STEPHANIE: Adzio – we can't . . . it's too dangerous.

ADZIO: More dangerous than waiting here, to see what happens to us?

STEPHANIE: I don't know.
The orphanage is my home.

ADZIO: I – I can't go on my own.
I need you.

STEPHANIE: Even if we managed to fight our way out of the Ghetto, where would we go?

ADZIO: You and me – you're clever – you're educated.
You can talk.
I can get by – I'm fly.

STEPHANIE: We make a team.

ADZIO: A team – yeah.
We could go to Russia – get a ship to New York.

STEPHANIE: America – to the country.

ADZIO: America.

STEPHANIE: And get a farm.

ADZIO: A bloody farm. Yeah.
No.
Farm? I want to get – a car.
In New York.

STEPHANIE: A farm and we'll grow vegetables, and cows and . . .

ADZIO: A car, and a smart suit and—

STEPHANIE: It won't happen . . .

ADZIO: It won't if we stay here.

STEPHANIE: Dr Korczak promised we'd be safe.

> . . .
> Wait.
> Let me wait one more day.
> Wait till tomorrow.
> Then I'll decide.

ADZIO: Well maybe I'll go alone.

STEPHANIE: I don't think you will.

ADZIO: How do you know?

STEPHANIE: Because . . .
> Because you've still got a lot of practising to do.
> Haven't you Fly?

**She kisses him.**

ADZIO: How'm I doing?

STEPHANIE: Five and a half.
> Keep working.

**She kisses him again.**

# Scene 21

**A blast of martial music from the radio.**

RADIO: This is a public health announcement.
> All Jews must gather at the railway yards tomorrow morning
> at 10 a.m. You will be taken to better accommodation in the
> east. I repeat.

**The ACTRESS turns the radio down a little.**

RADIO: This is a public health announcement.

All Jews must gather at the railway yards tomorrow morning at 10 a.m.

Anyone found in the Ghetto after this time will be executed on the spot.

ACTRESS: That evening, the chairman of the Ghetto, Adam Cerniakov was in his office. Already the Nazis had begun to deport people from the Ghetto. They were driven from their homes and crowded onto cattle trucks at a nearby railway yard. They were told they were going to camps in the countryside. Cerniakov had tried his best to keep people in Warsaw. He had specifically asked for an exemption for the orphans.

A Nazi officer came to see him.

**Nazi OFFICER enters Cerniakov's office.**

OFFICER: The second round of deportations begins tomorrow.

I trust you have arranged everything.

CERNIAKOV: As you said.

I have made the arrangements.

OFFICER: Good.

I want everyone on trains by one o'clock.

CERNIAKOV: All the people listed will be on the train.

But – I need to know.

What about the orphans?

OFFICER: Who?

CERNIAKOV: The orphans, the orphans – I spoke to your senior officer and he promised me he would consider an exemption for the orphans.

OFFICER: No exemptions.

CERNIAKOV: But – he – he said to me.

OFFICER: Look at me.
>How much do you think I care, old man?
>There are no exemptions.
>All of them on the train.

CERNIAKOV: Give me the telephone number for your head office in Berlin.
>Let me call them.

OFFICER: No exemptions.

CERNIAKOV: I won't do it.

OFFICER: You'll do it.
>Or you and your family will hang from the same rope.

**The OFFICER leaves.**
**The Cerniakov doll is in a chair. Broken.**

CERNIAKOV: Somebody bring me a glass of water, please.

**Water is brought.**

ACTOR: After the officer left, the chairman took a tablet of cyanide from his desk drawer. He swallowed it. He wrote two notes. One to his wife, apologising for leaving her. And the other to his fellow council members explaining that he could not hand over helpless children to the Germans. He saw no way out. He had lost all hope.
>When his friend, Dr Korczak, heard the news, he knew what it meant for the orphanage.

# Scene 22

**KORCZAK and the Soldier.**

KORCZAK: A cloudy morning.
    Five-thirty.
    It could be an ordinary day.
    Good morning, Soldier.
    I will look you in the eye and say good morning.
    Don't turn away.
    You are human.
    When a human greets another human
    At the beginning of the day
    He says good morning.
    . . .
    I'm listening.
    . . .
    At least I know that I'm human, Soldier
    With you – I can only guess.

# Scene 23

**STEPHANIE and ADZIO are looking out of the orphanage window.**

STEPHANIE: All those people.
    They have suitcases.
    Where are they going?

ADZIO: To the railway yard.
    The trains are taking them to the country.

STEPHANIE: It's like the whole Ghetto's leaving.
    Thousands.

ADZIO: We don't have time to watch.
   We have to run now.
   Before they come for us.

**STEPHANIE and ADZIO look for a way out.**

STEPHANIE: Get back in.
   There's a line of soldiers outside the back door.

ADZIO: Quick – try the other side.

**They do so.**

ADZIO: More soldiers.
   There's no way out.

STEPHANIE: Follow me.

# Scene 24

**The Nazi OFFICER comes into KORCZAK's office.**

OFFICER: Are you in charge?

**KORCZAK nods.**

OFFICER: All Jews out.
   All Jews out – now.

**KORCZAK prepares himself. He dresses up properly. Puts on a hat. Straightens his tie. He gathers the dolls into a marching formation.**

KORCZAK: Children.
   Gather together your things.
   Today we are going on a journey.

We will be taken to the country.
It might be a place a bit like Llittle Rose.
Where we used to go in summer.
Perhaps there will be pine trees.
And birds.
And fresh air.
We will march to the train together.
Under the orphanage flag.

**He produces the orphanage flag.**

A green flag.
Green to symbolise all things that grow.
Gather your things and line up under the flag.
Hold your heads up.
Backs straight.
Proud.

**KORCZAK takes a final look at the Soldier.**
**He takes his notebook from the desk and hides it under the floorboards.**

ACTOR: Then Dr Korczak hid his diary beneath the floorboards. In the hope that one day he might be able to come back for it. And went to lead the children on the march to the railway yard.

KORCZAK: This story happened.
It happened.

**Korczak forms the march.**
**He carries one child.**
**In the other hand he holds the flag.**
**The ACTOR and ACTRESS throw yellow armbands down on the stage in front of the march.**

ACTRESS: One witness who watched the children,
> In the intense summer heat,
> Singing their songs,
> Their heads high,
> Said —
> I shall never forget the scene as long as I live.
> This was no march to the train cars,
> But rather a silent protest against murder.
> A procession the like of which no human eye has ever seen before.

ACTOR: One story told is that, just as they boarded the train, a German soldier approached Dr Korczak with a signed document. A high ranking official had obtained a release for Korczak because of his famous work with children, his writing, and his ideas. The release was for Korczak alone.
> He refused it. And got onto the train.
> Another witness said that the children's yellow armbands thrown down onto the black cobbles looked like a field of buttercups.

# Scene 25

**The orphanage. STEPHANIE and ADZIO alone.**

STEPHANIE: Adzio, Adzio, there's a cupboard in here.

ADZIO: They'll find us.

STEPHANIE: Quiet.

ADZIO: I can hear them searching.

STEPHANIE: Shh.

ADZIO: Here they come.

SOLDIER'S VOICE: All Jews out. All Jews out.

STEPHANIE: Give me the knife.

ADZIO: What are you going to do?

**STEPHANIE opens the cupboard door.**
**She steps out with the knife.**
**Freeze.**

ACTOR: What happened next?

ACTRESS: Nobody who got on the train survived to tell what happened on their last journey. They were taken to Treblinka and they were all murdered.

ACTOR: Some people, like Adzio and Stephanie managed to escape the round-up and hid in the sewers of the Ghetto and in time they began an uprising against the Nazis.

ACTRESS: The uprising was defeated but,
like Adam Cerniakov,
like Korczak,
like the march of the children,
the uprising was an example,
that has become famous in history.
Because it showed that people would not accept the world the way the Nazis wanted it.

ACTOR: We invented the characters of Adzio and Stephanie,
but there were many like them in the Ghetto.
So what would have happened to them?
They almost certainly would have died fighting.
But who knows.
Perhaps they escaped — perhaps they went to America — perhaps —

**The KORCZAK actor relaxes his pose and becomes an actor again.**

KORCZAK ACTOR: Dr Korczak's works were discovered again after the war. And they became the basis for the United Nations Convention on the Rights of the Child. Many of the beliefs that he first put into practice in his orphanage are now accepted by international law.

These are the rights that Dr KORCZAK believed every child should have:

**The actors read from sheets which are then given to the audience as they leave.**

ACTORS: The right to love.

The right to respect.

The right to the best conditions to grow and develop.

The right to live in the present.

The right to be himself or herself.

The right to make mistakes.

The right to fail.

The right to be taken seriously.

The right to desire, and claim and ask.

The right to have secrets.

The right to respect for his or her possessions — however small.

The right to a court of his peers.

The right to a defence.

The right to commune with god.

The right to education.

The right to resist education.

The right to protest.

# End

# King Matt

# Stephen Greenhorn

### From the Author's Introduction

'*King Matt* was adapted from the novel, *King Matt the First* by Dr Korczak. He was a children's doctor in turn-of-the-century Poland who also saw service in the military. His radical ideas about the enpowerment and development of children were years ahead of his time. No plain theorist, he put his ideas into practice when he ran his own orphanage in Warsaw. It became a mini-republic for children, with its own parliament, court and newspaper. Much of this experience is reflected in the story of King Matt.

When the book was published it became a treasured piece of children's literature throughout eastern Europe. It is still held in the same kind of affection and regard as, say, *Alice in Wonderland* or *Peter Pan* are in this country. Like these it is a work which can be enjoyed by all ages. It has something important to say about the place of children in society, about the way adults treat them, about the responsibilities they are given and those they are denied. However, all of this is explored in a story which is breathtakingly paced and both funny and heartbreaking in turn.'

### Cast

A cast of 21 and extras, mix of male and female.

'Greenhorn has crafted a beautifully written and structured play, in a mixture of direct drama and powerful rhythmic verse narration that never loses its emotional momentum and keeps its young audience absorbed and involved throughout.'

*The Scotsman*

Available from www.fairplaypress.co.uk

# The Hard Man

# Tom McGrath & Jimmy Boyle

From the Introduction to the new edition by Phillip Breen

'As McGrath worked away on ideas and sketches for his new play, he began an extraordinary correspondence with one of Scotland's most notorious hard men, Jimmy Boyle. Boyle was an inmate at the special unit at Barlinne prison, serving a life sentence for murder; a crime he claimed he did not commit. The fascinating corres-pondence between the two formed the basis of the extraordinary and influential play-cum-bloody cabaret *The Hard Man*. It changed the life of McGrath and the face of Scottish theatre. It was the *Black Watch* of its day.'

From Thoughts on the first production by Peter Lichtenfels

'I didn't appreciate just how notorious Boyle was, and that every-body in Scotland seemed to hold strong opinions about him.'

Cast

A cast of 22, 15 male and 7 female.

'McGrath's best-known play, though, remains *The Hardman*, which premiered at the Traverse in 1977. Co-written with Jimmy Boyle, the Glasgow-born sculptor, writer and ex-criminal who had recently been released from prison after serving part of a life sentence, the play was an intense, stylised exploration of Boyle's early life, and of the cult of male violence on the streets of Glasgow.'

Joyce McMillan, *The Scotsman* May 2009

Available from www.fairplaypress.co.uk

# Egil Son of Nightwolf

# George Gunn

### Synopsis

An interpretation of the classic Icelandic *Egilssaga*

### From the Author's Introduction

'The idea of the setting of this play is that it takes place at a *ting*, a viking parliament or meeting, where the problems of the day were sorted out or at least discussed. As this play is taken from an Icelandic saga that would originally have been spoken or told, the idea is that this is what is happening, so the actors have to understand that they are addressing the audience and not necessarily each other, but at some points they will have to do this, obviously. A lot of the action takes place at sea and a lot of it takes place on the hoof. These people very rarely stood still.'

### Cast

A cast of 5, 3 male, 2 female and chorus.

'Drawing on Homer's story of the bereaved King Priam confronting his enemy Achilles, Cunneen vividly portraits the intensity of a senseless gang attack, the horror of a motiveless murder and the wider social causes and effects of knife crime. He does this in a way that strips away the banalities of naturalistic speech, using instead the heightened monologues of the Greeks to explore the human emotions generated by grand social forces.'

Mark Fisher, *The Guardian*

Available from www.fairplaypress.co.uk